ALL ALCOHOLICS ARE CHARMERS

Other books by Martina Evans

Poetry
THE INISCARRA BAR AND CYCLE REST

Fiction
MIDNIGHT FEAST
THE GLASS MOUNTAIN

Martina Evans

ALL ALCOHOLICS ARE CHARMERS

ANVIL PRESS POETRY

Published in 1998
by Anvil Press Poetry Ltd
Neptune House 70 Royal Hill London SE10 8RF

Copyright © Martina Evans 1998

This book is published with financial assistance
from The Arts Council of England

Set in Bembo by Anvil Press Poetry
Printed and bound in England
by Arc & Throstle Press, Todmorden, Lancs

ISBN 0 85646 304 3

A catalogue record for this book
is available from the British Library

FOR IRENE COTTER

ACKNOWLEDGEMENTS

Acknowledgements are due to the following publications where some of these poems have previously appeared: *Acumen, Cyphers, Developmental Medicine & Child Neurology, Force 10, The London Magazine, The New Statesman, Poetry Ireland Review, Poetry London Newsletter, Poetry News, Rialto.*

CONTENTS

Bacon and Cabbage

He said that it was a fact.
The whole field to be turned
into a small village
with our own roads, post office,
sweetshop to include toys.
No adults.
Their heads wouldn't get in the doors.
Brothers and sisters would live together
and never go off to get married.
The boys would go fishing
and the girls could come too,
if they didn't want to stay behind
baking apple tarts.
There would be no more bacon and cabbage.
No one would stand for it.
Connemara ponies would do all the work
and it would only take an hour a week.
I only had to send in my order
and my bed would be teeming with pups.
When I asked was it really really a fact,
he shouted. Had I not heard the priest
announce it off the altar on Sunday?
I hadn't because I never listened anyway.
But I couldn't believe
that Father O'Shea would make such final
　　　remarks
about bacon and cabbage.

First Holy Communion

The thing about having
a cross and chain was
you could run the chain
across your chin,
taste the metal
in your mouth.

It was the kind
of thing that older
girls did. Like
listening to Radio
Luxembourg or wearing
white knee highs
over Sunflower tights.

So what a lace-making
morning this was,
getting a silver cross
and chain,
shining in its own
bed of cotton wool.

I ran it across
my chin immediately,
put the cross in my mouth.
Heading up the road
with my white cup
overflowing,
white rosary beads
in white plastic
box. White new veil,
white knee high socks,
white soft strapped shoes,
white leather missal,

white dress that
did three sisters
and could have been
lacier, but anyway,
new three-tiered slip

– I'd have sung Waltzing Matilda
if I thought that I couldn't be heard –

only to arrive
at the altar
with bare thighs
smudging together
naked under the whole
shebang,
the shimmering
best pair ever
left in my bedroom
still wrapped
in their red-and-white
Roche's Stores bag.

Limbo

She said that she was sorry,
but it was hard
to take an interest in the world,
Heaven being such a fine place.

I, too, had been impatient,
hoping to sit on a needle,
the first minute
I came out of the confession box.
The needle would travel
straight and true (they said)
to pierce my heart
before my soul had a chance
to get stained again.

Just a bit of pain
and then the assumption
(wearing something soft and gauzy),
my bare feet sinking into clouds,
pink and blue and pinkish blue.
To Heaven.
To see *His* face.
The man who liked children,
sitting on the right hand
with a box of gold
Crunchies beside him.

They said that it was hard
on the crowd in limbo,
they never got to see
His Face.
But they could have everything else,

which must have included
dolls, pedal-cars, castles with
knee-high carpets, haystacks, snow.
Your own bedroom, including shelves,
sweets, tooth fairies, the Easter Bunny
and Santa, if you couldn't say that Santa was
      better
than Jesus, he had to be just as good.

The Outside

Christmas Eve
hung heavy.
Wide awake in our cold bedrooms,
blowing frosty towers of breath,
we dangled and drifted like wool
gathering on the edge of sleep.

Christmas morning,
staggering down the aisle,
six years old,
sick as an old man with a hangover,
sick from waiting
for Santa.

Outside, the wind would knock you,
the darkest morning,
carols at my back,
the high stone wall
and fir trees,
everlasting, vast and black.

The Black Priest

He came
to examine us in religion.
His skin wasn't black,
just the hair on his head,
the back of his neck,
his hands, his wrists.

His shaved chin blue
like a pirate's, he came
from an island,
some giant Irish-speaking
race that made him huge
and us helpless.

The sound of his name
an t-Athair Ó Súilleabháin
had a ring of wildness
to it, made us sit up.

It was hard to pretend
our normal indifference
with his big legs doubled up
in the nun's chair. Someone
next to me whispered that
his knees were like rockets.

But I didn't answer.
From where I was sitting
I could see Sister Lazarian,
an arrangement
of dark folds of cloth
in the corner, quivering,
waiting for one of us
to break out.

The Good Robber

An Ali Baba
of a Barbary pirate
of a chancer,
brown eyes,
brown hair,
swoop of Jewish nose,
brown chest,
white loincloth,
no nails,
just ropes
looping his hands
to the cross beam,
(they weren't *that* mad with him,
after all
he'd only stolen
things,
he'd never said
that he was great),
took his best chance
on Calvary
and was told
that he'd come up with
the password for Paradise.

The Mobile Library

It came once a fortnight
and I went under the beds,
scrabbling for overdue books,
balls of fluff as big as mice
skating across the linoleum.

It parked at the cross
for I don't know how long
and sometimes if I wasn't ready
with the books, I'd look out
and it would be gone.

Why didn't you warn me sooner?
I'd run out breathing anxious breaths
that tasted like frozen lemonade.

And that was the best thing,
when I was sure that it was still there,
my feet pressing into the deep steps.

Smoke

Every Saturday
on their way to confessions,
they peered through the piano teacher's
letterbox.

The older girls said
that the piano was still standing
but she could see nothing,
only black cobwebs hanging.

She found it hard to move away
from the letterbox, searching
through the small rectangle,
taking in that terrible smell.

Was it true that the teacher
went out playing,
flame-tipped fingers racing away?

Years later
the schoolgirl was a nurse,
remembered the piano teacher
when another burnt woman
was brought in half dead.

They said that it must have been
a cigarette that went on burning
between dead-drunk fingers.

Alcohol dropped into her veins
from a drip, protecting
her from delirium tremens
while they dressed the burns.

The drink-soaked body
was a melting instrument,
the nurses' fingers
ran up and down the scales.

Afterwards
the nurse scrubbed herself for days,
the notes of the screams still close
in her ears,
but the smell was like smoke,
she couldn't wipe it.

One Evening in July

From a convent
to the boat,
and straight down
to Ward's in Piccadilly
with my big sister.

I was sitting on a barrel,
when a Glaswegian beckoned
and I leaned forward
while he whispered
in my ear.

Something good
I didn't doubt, weren't
the Scots and the Irish
mad about each other?

I'm looking forward
to the twelfth, he said.
I nodded knowingly.
I'm going over
for the twelfth, he said
again and I tried to
think of something
encouraging.

The weather might hold out,
I said. Listen, here, Fenian
bitch, he said and I put my
hand over my mouth.
I'm going over to kill
your brothers and sisters.

But my family don't live
in the North, I said,
whipping him up when
it was the last thing
I wanted to do.

I thought the Fenians were all dead,
I said, nearly put my hand out
to feel that he wasn't a ghost.

Papist was the next weird
word he came out with
and he ran out
looking awful upset
before I had time to tell
him that I'd just recently
become an atheist.

Stories

I'm biased
describing your eyes
as blue and gold,
but over your father's
shoulder I can see
one huge blue-gold orb,
charcoal eyebrow drawn
in utter belief,
reeled into his spiel
about boyhood in Bantry.
Wily cats stepping aside
at waterfalls,
foolish fateful dogs,
lakes forests and fishing,
men with drink hidden
in their caps.

Then you begin your story,
reaching for the words
that he dropped like coins
from his pocket.
His landscape is yours now,
wily cats, waterfalls, dogs
whiskey in your cap.
Everything powdered with star
colours and Christmas scarlet,
one blue-gold eye opened wide,
in this first floor city flat.
I haven't felt so good
since you or was it he
said he liked my eyes.
Said they were brown and silver.

Cows

are mostly silent,
sharp-shouldered,
fertile,
moist-eyed,
long-lashed,
cream-coloured,
or black,
or black and white,
or brown,
or brown and white,
or red,
or red and white
(white with red ears
the ones from the
underworld),
motherly,
slow-walking,
vegetarian,
horny
and gentle,
all women dread
to be called
cows.

The Wide World

He loves racing,
Cheltenham, Ascot,
Leopardstown, Mallow,
Newmarket, Tralee
and Galway.

I like it here.
The kitchen smell.
Quiet. Peppers, apple.
The kitchen table
scored with lines
from my knife.

Garlic, fennel, onions.

When we first met
the sky was blue flames
over Montenotte.

Now I like feeling rested,
waking up when the morning
is not spoilt. Paperbacks propped
against saucepans, no rain
inside my collar or shoe.

Potato, tomato, thyme.

I could have gone
to the races too.
Risked the blue flames,
the comets,
the hangovers.

Kentucky, bluegrass, racing.

Cigarette

Around the end
of November
I'm filled
with desire
for a pure strong
inhalation
of impurity,
each gasp
a disappointment
which leads me
to toothpaste
and soap.
And it won't
go away,
it breathes
through my skin,
clinging
like a fatal mistake.
Two stony angels
open wrought-iron
gates of guilt,
my heart is empty
and loud,
as if I've been done
for murder.
But oh
the yellow-skinned
gypsy life of a smoker!
Blue wreathes
join like puzzles,
wafting back
the scents of older Christmases,
whiskey and pine,

heavy longing,
night-light
conversations
stretching into
ashy mornings.

The Shop

If only they sold
bottles of sleep
in shades of wandering green,
grey and open blue,
stacked in shops
with sliding shelves
and cloudy windows.
You could drift
into that kind of shop,
lean against
the hammocky counter
and call for a pint.
Or a six-pack to take away.
Even a half a pint.
Just pour me a half a cup,
a whiskey measure,
a thimble
or even a drop on my raging finger.
Anything to quench
my desperation
down among the restless flames,
hanging out with Macbeth
and the thirsty mothers.

The Cure

I have the cure
for insomnia.
Give into it,
don't paddle.
I let my raft
out on the rush
of the ocean,
imagine the most
embarrassing things
I can think of and
then imagine
even worse. Doorways,
corners, irreversible
disgrace.
I stop blushing,
in no time at all
I'm so bored
with my wickedness,
I begin to slide,
the roar of the waters
of Holloway grows dim
outside my window,
a laid-back devil laughs,
pressing down on my eyelids
with long white fingers,
sleep is down in a heavy curtain.

The Waves

As quick as the needle
the opiate ran in.
Like kindly attendants
at a hanging
the nurses came with
open-backed gown,
flimsy paper hat,
long white stockings.
The razor fear
brushed against me,
missed the crests
and iced the dips.
Supine on a trolley,
floating down white walls,
approaching the waves
of theatre, through
rollers as high as
Victorian tombs,
knowing happiness
is a drug that blood
won't hold and my heart
is big
as big and as bright
as this room.

Labyrinth

The Eustachian tube
joins
the ear
and the pharynx,
so delicate,
so slippy,
so easy
for infection.
There's an ocean
in the ear,
blood beats,
pounds,
mimics the sea,
the sea.
Down in
the crimson deep
the semicircular
canals
are arranged
in different
planes,
liquid and balance
in a maze,
a quiet centre
rose coloured.
Noiseless
not even
the lightest lapping
lapping.
There's a world
in the ear,
so delicate,
so strange,
like silence.

Mysteries

I don't know
who lives in
these neighbouring
streets. At dawn
each wall is a strange
cat, this basement with
purple blue curtains,
that flat, smooth white
painted shutters,
this flower box,
glimpse of bookcase,
candles, mirrors, milk
carton on a wood table,
the smell of spices
like a resurrection
at five o'clock,
this curry,
these people
partaking of perfect
food I can only imagine.

Charity

Up and down
the Holloway Road,
scarlet veins
on their faces,
royal purple noses,
trousers pitched
above their ankles,
roaming through
The Half Moon,
The Mulberry Tree,
The Enterprise,
The Whittington Hospital.

Rakish debonair
remarks about racing
and matches.
The most ironic
of men *Hi over here*
we are in the
winner's enclosure!

Walk past the jokes
the cracked bells
of laughter.
We've got to shrug
each other off.
Whether or not
money has been pressed
into broken
and healed
sandpaper fists.

The Drum and Monkey

You're a right rake,
the nurse said. I said
It's hard to keep white
raincoats spotless,
and you'd never think
I was seventy.

See the multiple healed
fractures on his ribs,
years of falling and fighting,
one of your countrymen
is he?

How many times did
he get up again?
the nurse asked the air.
and I'd swear that she
was impressed.
I threw back my
shoulders like a man.

Wedges of new bone formation.
Telltale, the doctor
was droning like a priest,
like a man who couldn't
get enough of his voice.

Oh no nurse, I said
in front of him.
Oh no nurse
never touch a drop,
only the wance
I had a half pint
of shandy and landed

in jail for a night oh
that finished me rightly
with the drink
oh god no nurse!

On my way out
the doctor was
still nosing the old
X-ray, I hit the nurse
one tip on the shoulder.
Any chance, I said.
Any chance you'd meet
me for wan?
Any evening.
Just call into
the Drum and Monkey,
Junction Road.
I'll be sitting up
at the counter.
Waiting.

All Alcoholics
Are Charmers

All alcoholics
are charmers
my mother said
that is if
they're any good.
How else would
they get away
with it?
Your father
for instance.
Don't mention
my father
I said,
he's had a
terrible sad life.
Listen to that
for twisting,
she said,
I was the one
with the
terrible sad life.
How could he have
had the time for it?
When he was on the
road day and night.

All alcoholics
are charmers.
If they're any good.
That's how they get
away with it.

My father wore a soft
grey overcoat
with a soaking smell
of smoke and whiskey.
Made me want
to hang onto it
like a blanket.
When he was dying
my mother was always
crying and waving
a bottle of Black Bushmills
just out of his reach.

All alcoholics
are charmers.
My father gave up
the drink
every single Lent,
no matter how
they coaxed.
You can say
what you like,
you can nail me
to the cross,
he said,
nothing
will persuade me
to take anything
stronger
than a good warm glass
of Sandyman's Port Wine.

Set Dancing

The knee is rightly gone, too much dancing. Aye.
The swinging did it. I swang and I swang.
I was at it every night of the week, sure the old knee
    gave in.
You think they look good in Kerry?
It's all that sliding makes 'em look good.
It's all slides and polkas in Kerry, reels in Clare.
Do you think it'll ever get better? Do you?
Aye, I'll have to give it up.
Did I hear you say gentle exercise?
Now you're talking, now we're burning coal.
I walk up to Ryan Cabs of an evening, back down
Tufnell Park Road and over to Archway, five times a
    day.
Is it fifteen miles? Is it?
But I'll never dance again, I think it's a cartilage. Do
    you?
Aye, I hear it crunching inside, sixteen weeks now on
    Tuesday.
I'll have to give up the dancing.
Would you not think so?
I only took it up to cure my back. Whiplash is a right
    bugger, so it is.
I'll tell you a good cure for it now, go into a room on
    your own.
Stand on your head with your legs up against the wall.
Let the blood down into you, send the oxygen ahead.
Do you believe me? You'll stretch that neck like an
    elastic band.
You'll use muscle you never used before. Do you
    believe me now?
You'll have a big red head full of oxygen on you.
Am I talking bull's wool? Am I? I worked it out
    myself.

I heard about the oxygen on the radio.
Would you believe me now?
Am I a right eedjit? Am I?
I'm not, am I?
Aye, but there's no cure for the old whiplash.
If I'd any hope of dancing again! Sixteen weeks on
    Tuesday.
Aren't I a right cripple? Aren't I? Fifty-five imagine!
I'm like an old horse you'd see out in the paddock.
'Twas the constant swinging on top of that old knee.
Rightly gone, aye. You don't agree? Why not?
Get away out of that! You'll make a right fool out of me.
I put the tin hat on top of myself rightly with those sets.
You're only trying to get away from me, now, so you are.
You are. I don't blame you.
My wife's gone off her game, sure, sixteen weeks now on
    Tuesday,
but I'd give my right eye, so I would, to have my knee
    back,
swinging around the old dance floor.

Young Mayo Men

They're like something
out of *Vogue*, I said
and I was told to put on my glasses.
High noon in Holloway,
they're digging the roads.

Inside, I'm reading
The Soul of Man Under Socialism
by Oscar Wilde.
I've begun to leave the flat
by different routes, I can't bear
the shyness of us all.

How bad would Oscar
have felt, would he
have felt each shovel sound
like a blade in his side?

Oscar would have wanted
to do beautiful things with them.
He would not have wanted
to rush out and say *for god's sake
give me that shovel.*

The Mayo accent is being hurled
around under my window, I can't
understand most of it. All I can
make out is the soft-looking one
getting a bit riled
saying over and over
What does it matter?

Christmas Days

for P. D.

After Mass, he was at the gate.
I don't know who he was.
He might have been one of the brothers dressed up.
1949. We all went down to the gate, right?
I was given a big box, I couldn't believe it.
Inside the box, lovely box,
I opened it, train carriages, you know, with the tracks.
Now, right?
And we got our presents and we opened it.
And then the brothers said, now boys, time for your
    dinner.
Line up, please.
Christmas dinner on the table.
When we came back the presents weren't there.
We never saw them no more.
I only saw it for ten minutes.
I never seen it no more.
The next year.
It was brushes and a bucket.
And all little colours, yellow, pink, orange.
This was 1950. It was in a set,
big brushes, that length,
all little bottles full of colours, red and blue.
That was 1950. Same thing happened, went to your
    dinner.
Never saw it again, never seen it no more.
1951, one of the boys said and one of the brothers heard
    him
we won't see this no more.
He got a hiding, a good hiding.
He was put to bed wrapped in a mackintosh
    with no food.

That was what they did to me when I wet my trousers
    in Benediction.
They put me to bed for a day in a mackintosh.
It was sort of red-looking.
They took the sheets and blankets off the bed.
That was 1951.
I still remember the carriages I was given.
And the tracks. 1949.
I was trying to use the paints.
We left our presents all on the table.
We never saw them no more.
That's true. Where did they go?
Did they sell them or what?
I'm talking about the '40s here.
We seen it, they were new all right, they were brand
    new.
But where did they go?
Where did the train set go in 1950?
Paints, the tubes, the little colours, red, orange and all?
After Mass every Christmas Day, Santa Claus down at
    the gate.
We all rushing down to the gate. Here's Santie, right?
Everyone's queueing up at the gate, right?
You go to your Christmas dinner, that day.
And where did they go from the table?
Who took them while we were having our Christmas
    dinner?
We never see them no more.
We never see them no more.

The Pet

It's a tonic to see you, so it is, now I mean that.
James hardly ever talks about you and I'm mad to know
    everything.
It's all Grainne with him. Didn't you know? Oh god, yes.
Grainne this, Grainne that, Grainne's extension, Grainne's
    operation.
That's not fair, to you. I mean that. Is it now?
To treat your children like that, now, my heart goes out
    to you.
Going on about the one child the whole time.
Going back and back to the one child, like a boomerang
    gone wallop.
Every one of my grandchildren (and I've got eleven of
    them) gets the same present every Christmas.
Four pound ninety nine pence worth of something, and I
    have to be cute about it.
They're watching like hawks the whole time.
What did Diarmuid get? What did Sara get? What! What!
    What!
How much, how much, four pound ninety-nine pence.
Sometimes I do have to go over and above.
Donal doesn't like cheap things for the children and you
    can't blame him.
Isn't the whole world smothering under plastic?
The girls are the worst, though. They're like foxes.
They say Donal is my pet and he's getting the pub.
Isn't he the only boy?
They're like hens fighting in the yard.
They say, well, I suppose he is my only boy, that I'm
partial, but I can't cut the business into five pieces, can I?
But I am really, a small biteen partial, he is my one and
    only, he *is* my favourite.

Emergency Stop

You'd want to be a topper here
with your emergency stops,
the old darkies are reckless.

Christ Almighty! I'm glad
to be getting out of it,
they've Axminster Road
ruined, 'twas all Irish once,
now there's these pups
with hoods, ripping purses,
have you seen the way
they do their hair?
No meaning to it at all.

What? The road's looking better?
Sure, they've nothing else to do,
only their gardens, they won't
take a job for love or money.

Don't get me wrong, like,
I love the Africans, they send
their children to the best of schools.
It's those fecking West Indians,
they won't lift a finger.

Slavery? Will you stop codding me.
It's we're the slaves, paying for those
cars, nothing smaller than a bulk tank
will do them.

I'd a lovely job last week,
collecting a crowd of Mullingar cattle
business men from the airport,
bringing them down to Surrey.

I didn't see a black or a Chink
or a Paki for the whole day,
the nicest people you could meet
in Surrey!
You're getting out *here?*
Easy, easy now.
You'll give us all a heart attack.
Jaysus, that's the handle of my
door that you've just thrown down
on the road. Hi! Stop,
ya blackguard! Ya Cork jade!

The Black Cab

From the moment he sat down
she knew that he was there,
his yellow death's-head
smiling among the steamy-wet
pile of out-patients.

She prayed that she wouldn't get him.

As the afternoon wore through
the shuffling crowd, she feared
that every name she called
would unfold him from his seat.

And she got him in the end,
had to feel the zygomatic arches
under his waxy-skinned cheeks,
stare close into his eyes
as she adjusted his skull.

He never took his smiling eyes
from her face, talking about
the accident,
the drunk and drugged girls,
how she was only seventeen,
the one who came crashing
through his windscreen,
to sit up dead on his lap.

The Treatment for Cancer
of the Lip

It was a radioactive implant,
a big square thing
like a chunk of tobacco
sewn into the lower lip.

Old-fashioned smokers
of clay pipes,
now a radioactive source,
had to be kept away
from everyone else,
they fogged X-ray films
and frightened children.

What did they think
these men in flat caps
with their sulky lips,
banished to corners
far away from
Clarke's Number One Plug,
Erinmore, Condor
and Cherokee,
to this place
without fire or smoke,
nothing to cut and shape,
or press and hold,
not even a dog for company?

The Smell

It wasn't bad,
just sweet and dry
and musty like old one-bar
heaters and small parlours,
like singed hair or burnt jam.

It seemed to come from
the folds of his tweed
clothes, or his hands,
his pores, the back of his neck,
but really you couldn't
pin it down.

He'd had bad sinuses for years,
they were a bit painful, alright,
but he was a great believer in Vicks.

On the X-ray
it was a honeycomb of a cancer,
eating away the bones of his face,
no one had seen the like,
an excited doctor ran past
the brown-coated diffident figure,
an interesting case,
no one asked about the pain.

The Last Picture

She would get special dispensation
to go back in a dream.

There would be no stains
on her uniform, white
as wedding-cake icing.

Down the long corridor, her patient would wait.

An 'immigration chest',
a routine X-ray
to satisfy the Canadian authorities.

A square gleaming on his back,
a cross falling precisely
on the ninth thoracic vertebra.

Breathe in and hold it.
The sound of the anode rotating
like a small man on a bicycle
pedalling furiously
inside the X-ray tube.
Breathe away.

Clavicles equidistant,
scapulas out of the way
of the lung fields, the film
neither too dark, nor too pale.

All her past mistakes would be rubbed out.

She would have time to sit in a glow
as his feet tapped away,
his white heart
and perfectly positioned bones
pegged on the illuminated viewer.

Peace

Doors shut and cars drive away.
I switch off all the radios triumphantly.
Make the coffee.

The big warm room,
sun on the snow on the mountains.

The fire puffs, the dogs sigh
draping and draping
their liver and white bodies.

The window is the cover of a book,
cattle, pockets of sun trapped in green,
cottages scribbling smoke.

Each irregular field holds its emerald
misty tale to its chest, the sun, snow,
the lime and gold and violet intensity,

all a calf's gentle breath away from loneliness.

Before the Magi

Letting the dog off the lead,
up to the gallery
and down to the front of the altar,
leaning in like a robber
to weigh the Infant Jesus
in my arms.

The best thing to be
was a shepherd with a soft lamb
draped round my shoulders,
kneeling down beside
the cow, the donkey,
letting their breaths
warm my ankles,
sinking into the straw
and the smell of it.

Cows, babies, sheep and shepherds
made the best toys. Donkeys too.
A dark green cave close to the altar
full of mystery figures wearing cloaks
and tunics, the dog raising
woofs to the rafters, something
she didn't like about the stand
of Saint Joseph.

Cat in the Toyshop

He swiped his head
against your dress
and we thought that
he was the crown
of this sky blue morning
that unfurled toys
under a floating ceiling
of paper lanterns
turning our heads
round and round.
But his tail swung
like a skipping rope,
and he sank
his red angry scrawl
into your small plush
hand, watched your
crushed retreat,
vertical slit eyes
glowing behind
the red and green
glass beads you
thought were treasure.
You said
that you'd never
go back.
Then we began
telling people
and you rippled back
recounting
that orange and black
striped story.
With fangs.

Fairy Cakes

Stopping on Regent's Park Road
we found a man from the Punjab,
in a navy black beard,
feeding two blonde women
from behind the counter
of his own newsagents.

They leaned against the photocopier,
dropping crumbs, moaning things
like *stop* and *no more*,
but he only smiled.

He'd packets and packets of them
stacked up behind him; we circled
the counter beaming at the image
of a villain from an Indian movie.

Although not usually a good
eater, my daughter wolfed hers,
paid it her highest compliment,
too much sugar.

Clockwork

Her body is a sweet
and terrible clock ticking
in the slight triangles
of the scapulas
winged to her back,
veins running like
indigo ink under her skin.
I take her head
in my two big hands,
she asks me to put my ear
to the string bones
of her chest, check
that her heart is still going.

The Mystery of Shoes

I avert my eyes passing
shoeshops
but the devil
peers out, ruby eyes
illuminating
a window in Venice
filled with expensive colours
of chocolate, donkey, desert.
Mary Magdalene unbuckling
Jesus's dusty sandals,
all those people in the bible
showing off their toes,
the gleaming shoes
my daughter begged for,
smart as paint,
strapped to her feet,
they made her shy,
so chic she was afraid
that they'd speak to her.

Dream Houses

Over and over,
we draw rosy cottages
and stony farmhouses
right beside the bold
Atlantic.

Candle- and bat-filled caves
with round windows,
brown-eyed seals
clustered at the entrance,
beyond the pet hare
and the arctic fox.

Sometimes it's tall tall
town houses, with balconies,
attics, cellars,
the sound of the sea
in the trees all around.

These houses grow inside us.

I dreamt of a house in Holloway
in a circle of mountains,
a green ocean washing the front door.

My daughter talks
of a house with a stream
running right through the middle,
the Salmon of Knowledge
lepping for joy inside.

His Master's Teeth

This Chinese puppeteer
with prominent teeth
has the look
of a North Cork bowler.

Country men
had irresistible smiles,
lips that just wouldn't
stay down over their teeth.

Strong arms swinging
round like millwheels,
the mad run down
sighing country roads,
the bawl of spectators,
the whisper of bets.

This delicate puppet
dances with elegantly
jointed hands and knees,
it's old old painted face
moving under the twitching
fingers, twitching lips.

NOTE: *Bowling* (pronounced to rhyme with
howling) is an ancient Irish game played
along country roads in Cork and Armagh.
The small metal bowl is thrown along the
road and there's a lot of gambling on the
winner, that is whoever gets to the finishing
point in the smallest number of throws.

Chinese words, Chinese
songs running alongside
the vowels of men
from Banteer, Kanturk,
Bweeng and Dromahane.

The surge of trees and voices,
Good man, Christy!
the rustle of twenty- and fifty-
pound notes.

The Grey Mare

i.m. Thomas Cotter 1900–1979

After the Truce,
his prison letter
was all about
his dream about
her.

Coming first
in the mare and brood class
at Newcastle,
his bursting pride
leading her into the ring
with colours up.

Afterwards,
awake in the cell,
his fear for her leg
was stronger
than his hope
for 'a grand and glorious peace'.

She was the first one he called on
the night of his escape.

In the seventies
he was an old fighter,
the same age as the century,
hook nose,
burnt brown eyes,
whiskey head,
tobacco fingers.

Yellow riding boots
with elasticated sides,
morning or evening,
wedding or funeral,
always on his feet.

He was ready for her,
the day she'd come again
drumming her hooves.

A Quiet Man

i.m. Richard Cotter 1902–1988

He was a quiet man,
a secret man, who liked to be alone,
and he had ten children.

He couldn't bear to cut down his trees.

Every Christmas he defiantly brought in
the worst pine, with the scantiest branches,
and his family spent the whole Christmas
trying to cover it up.

Passionate about fires, inside or out,
he spent summer evenings tending crowds
of them in a field full of sunset.

He was a warm small-eyed man,
his hands were big,
his forever young pink-and-white skin
his crowning glory.

He could sing,
a fine dry note,
pucking out rebellious words.

He was a quiet man
though he'd kill for his dog.

He was a joker and a cod
and it was easy for him,
with all about him flapping their mouths
like multicoloured scarves in the wind.

He was a careful man,
though it could be construed as meanness:
'No fear *he*'d ever turn into an alcoholic!'

He liked Rum and Butter toffees, cherry brandy,
Sandyman's Port poured with a heavy hand,
tapping his broad fingers on the table.

His wife and children's mad grand sweeping
talk flew around the house like magic carpets.
He smiled and tapped and sipped.

He was a quiet man,
we could sit in a room,
the two of us,
with no talk.

New and Recent Poetry from Anvil